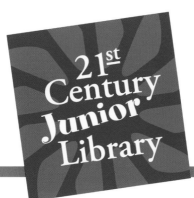

21st Century Junior Library

WORKING AT A GROCERY STORE

by Katie Marsico

CHERRY LAKE PUBLISHING * ANN ARBOR, MICHIGAN

Published in the United States of America by Cherry Lake Publishing
Ann Arbor, Michigan
www.cherrylakepublishing.com

Content Adviser: Sharon Castle, PhD, Associate Professor of Elementary Social Studies, George Mason University, Fairfax, VA

Reading Consultant: Cecilia Minden-Cupp, PhD, Literacy Specialist and Author

Photo Credits: Cover and page 4, ©iStockphoto.com/sjlocke; page 6, ©Cultura/Alamy; page 8, ©iStockphoto.com/sjlocke; cover and page 10, ©iStockphoto.com/Joas; page 12, ©UpperCut Images/Alamy; cover and page 14, ©iStockphoto.com/Thomas_EyeDesign; page 16, ©JUPITERIMAGES/Creatas/Alamy; page 18, ©iStockphoto.com/quach; cover and page 20, ©sonya etchison, used under license from Shutterstock, Inc.

LIBRARY OF CONGRESS CATALOGING-IN-PUBLICATION DATA
Marsico, Katie, 1980–
 Working at a grocery store / by Katie Marsico.
  p. cm.
Includes index.
ISBN-13: 978-1-60279-265-4
ISBN-10: 1-60279-265-8
1. Grocery trade—Juvenile literature. 2. Supermarkets—Juvenile
literature. I. Title.
HD9320.5.M37 2009
381'.41023—dc22   2008007552

Cherry Lake Publishing would like to acknowledge the work of
The Partnership for 21st Century Skills.
Please visit www.21stcenturyskills.org for more information.

CONTENTS

Good cashiers are nice to customers.

What Is a Grocery Store?

You are in a store that has lots of food. Your cart is full. You are ready to pay for your **groceries**. A **cashier** smiles at you. He asks you to step over to his **cash register**. He is one of the many grocery store workers who help you do your grocery shopping.

Some workers can tell you about fruits and
vegetables you have not tried before.

A grocery store is where people go to buy food. They also buy other everyday items there. Do you go shopping with your parents? What does your family like to buy?

Many people do lots of different jobs in grocery stores. They all work together so you can get what you need. Let's take a look at some grocery store workers.

Make a Guess!

Guess how many people work at your local grocery store. Write down your guess. Ask a worker for an exact number the next time you go shopping. Was your guess correct?

One section of a grocery store has different kinds of meat.

Grocery Store Workers

Have you noticed that there are different **sections** in a grocery store? One section may have baked goods such as breads and cakes. Another might have cheese and milk. Each section has workers to help you.

Bakers make bread. They also make cakes and other sweet treats.

Butchers slice meat for you to take home. You can talk to a baker if you want to order a birthday cake. A **produce** worker might help you decide what kind of apples to buy.

Who else works in a grocery store? **Stock clerks** place food and other items on shelves. Cashiers tell you how much money everything in your cart costs. They take your money and put it in the cash register. A **bagger** puts your groceries in bags or boxes while you pay the cashier.

Some grocery stores are very big. Managers help things run smoothly.

Who is in charge of these workers? A different **manager** usually takes care of each section of the store. Managers **train** the workers in their section. They also order supplies. They must make sure that items in their section are fresh and ready to buy.

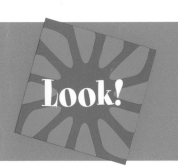

Look!

Look around the next time you go grocery shopping. Try to spot workers in sections that have not been named. Hint: you might see them in the frozen food section. How many sections does your grocery store have?

Store managers are happy to answer any
questions that customers have.

The store manager runs the entire grocery store. She hires other workers. She tries to come up with new ways to increase sales. The store manager talks to shoppers, too. She wants people like you to be happy and come back!

You can see that it takes many workers to run a grocery store. Each one tries to make shopping easy and fun for you and your family.

Grocery store workers usually wear aprons or uniforms. This helps customers know that they work in the store.

Do You Want to Work at a Grocery Store?

Would you like to work in a grocery store someday? You can start getting ready now! Talk to workers the next time you go shopping. Find out what they like best about their jobs.

Grocery lists help you remember what you need to buy.

You may learn that many grocery store workers enjoy helping people and working with food. Most grocery store workers are also organized. They must remember where lots of different items are.

Are you organized? Ask your parents if you can help write the grocery list each week. Make a note if you see that you are running out of a certain food. Check off items on your list the next time you go shopping.

Many people work in grocery stores. Maybe some day you will work in a grocery store, too!

A grocery store can be an exciting place to work. Find out as much as you can now. This is the best way to decide if one of the jobs you have just read about is right for you!

Ask Questions!

Do you know some of the workers at your grocery store. Ask them about their jobs. Find out how they learned to do their jobs. Asking questions will help you find out about jobs that interest you.

GLOSSARY

bagger (BAG-gur) a worker who puts groceries in bags or boxes for customers

cash register (KASH REH-jiss-tur) a machine that cashiers use to store money and add up shoppers' bills

cashier (kah-SHEER) a worker who adds up what shoppers owe and accepts their payment before they leave the store

groceries (GRO-sur-ees) food and other everyday items you buy in a store

manager (MAH-ni-jer) a person who is in charge of certain sections of the grocery store or the entire store itself

produce (PROH-duse) fresh fruits and vegetables

sections (SEK-shuhnz) parts of something

stock clerks (STAHK CLURKZ) workers who arrange food and other items on store shelves

train (TRAYN) to teach someone a skill

FIND OUT MORE

BOOKS

Kishel, Ann-Marie. *Cashier.* Minneapolis: Lerner Publishing Group, 2007.

Leeper, Angela. *Grocery Store.* Chicago: Heinemann Library, 2004.

WEB SITES

PBS Kids—Supermarket Adventure

pbskids.org/arthur/games/supermarket/index.html
Play a grocery store game

Supermarket Sports Activity Sheet—Fun Games for Kids

www.sunkist.com/kids/games/safari.asp
Print out a sheet of fun games to play on your next trip to the grocery store

INDEX

ABOUT THE AUTHOR

Katie Marsico is the author of more than 30 children's books. She lives in Elmhurst, Illinois, with her husband and two children. She would especially like to thank the staff at the Jewel-Osco on Schiller Street in Elmhurst for helping her research this title.